Sharing Religious Education

A brief introduction to the possibility of an
inclusive approach to Religious Education in
Northern Ireland

Norman Richardson

Northern Ireland

RE Today Services, a part of Christian Education, is an ecumenical educational charity which works throughout the United Kingdom.
Its aims are:

• to support religious education in schools
• to increase awareness of the spiritual, moral, social and cultural dimensions of the curriculum
• to articulate Christian perspectives on education.

RE Today Services is committed to the teaching of the major world faiths in religious education, and to an accurate and fair representation of their beliefs, values and practices in all its teaching materials. RE Today Services fulfils these aims:

• by publishing teaching materials, a termly magazine *REtoday* and distributing the *British Journal of Religious Education*
• by offering professional development and consultancy services through its professional staff
• by arranging national and regional courses for teachers, pupils and others interested in education
• by research and curriculum development work
• by sponsoring the work of the National Association of Teachers of RE (NATRE).

Acknowledgement
This publication has received financial support from the Northern Ireland Community Relations Council which aims to promote a pluralist society characterised by equity, respect for diversity and recognition of interdependence. RE Today gratefully acknowledges their support. However, the views expressed in this publication do not necessarily reflect those of the Community Relations Council or of RE Today Services.

Community Relations Council

Designed and typeset by: eplsdesign.com

Published by: Christian Education Publications, 1020 Bristol Road, Selly Oak, Birmingham, B29 6LB, in association with CEM Northern Ireland.

ISBN 978-1-905893-93-5

A CIP Catalogue record for this book is available from the British Library.

Printed and bound in the UK by:
Think PA Ltd, P&A House, Alma Road, Chesham, Buckinghamshire, HP5 3HB

In memory of Dr John Greer (1932–96) of the University of Ulster, who inspired the author and many other teachers of RE in Northern Ireland to think and teach beyond the confines of traditional expectations.

All schools should ensure, through their policies, structures and curriculae, that pupils are consciously prepared for life in a diverse and inter-cultural society and world.
A Shared Future: Policy and Strategic Framework for Good Relations in Northern Ireland (OFMDFM, 2005)

Those who teach about religions and beliefs should have a commitment to religious freedom that contributes to a school environment and practices that foster protection of the rights of others in a spirit of mutual respect and understanding among members of the school community.
Toledo Guiding Principles on Teaching about Religions and Beliefs in Public Schools (OSCE/ODIHR 2007)

Contents

Introduction

My fundamental belief in writing this booklet is that inclusive, fair and balanced religious education should be an important element of school education in a democratic society. Some people may regard a plural or diverse society as uncomfortable and even threatening, particularly in relation to religious belief and practice, but I believe that in such a society there are exciting opportunities for developing positive awareness, deepened understanding and new relationships. This is especially important in a society like Northern Ireland which is perceived to be divided along religious-cultural lines, and in such a context the role of the teacher of Religious Education becomes very important.

Schooling in Northern Ireland remains significantly separate – over 90 per cent of children attend schools that serve their own perceived community, usually labelled by the religious terminology of 'Catholic' or 'Protestant'. The teaching of religion is a major factor in this educational separateness, along with other issues relating to the differing religious identities associated with the two largest school systems. Since the 1980s a growing sector of Integrated Schools has emerged, currently serving around 7 per cent of the school-going population, and more recently schools from the two separate systems have been encouraged to develop collaborative schemes and joint facilities as part of the process of building a shared future. Yet, even in these more 'mixed' environments, Religious Education remains a contentious and often-avoided area of the curriculum, and teachers may feel very uncertain about how to deal with it.

This document grew out of an in-service seminar organised by the Northern Ireland Council for Integrated Education (NICIE) for RE teachers from the integrated schools, both primary and secondary, in November 2002, and since that time has been updated every so often for use mainly with students and serving teachers. The current version continues to refer primarily to RE in Northern Ireland,[1] though it may well be perceived to be relevant elsewhere, not least where religious division and diversity may challenge traditional approaches to the teaching of religion in schools. Internationally the issuing of advice and guidance on religious teaching in a human rights context from bodies such as the Council of Europe, UNESCO and the Organisation for Security and Co-operation in Europe (OSCE) has lent credibility to some of the discussions here and has highlighted both the potential and the challenge of teaching religion in public schools in plural societies.

I offer the reflections and suggestions in this booklet as a contribution to the discussion on how Religious Education may make a positive contribution to a more inclusive and shared Northern Ireland. In that sense it is a vision statement, a position paper, and it invites a response. Part of the discussion inevitably focuses on the disadvantages of educational separation, but while this seems to me to be a regrettable feature of schooling in Northern Ireland, there appears to be no immediate prospect of establishing a single system. Thus the challenge here is to all kinds of schools – separate or mixed, diverse or monocultural – to consider how they can contribute to a more shared religious education.

I am grateful to all those who have helped me to shape these thoughts, and particularly to my colleague, James Nelson, for his helpful observations, suggestions and continuing encouragement.

Norman Richardson,
Stranmillis University College, Belfast BT9 5DY
n.richardson@stran.ac.uk
January 2014

---

1   Readers unfamiliar with the schooling and RE situation in Northern Ireland are recommended to the website of the European Forum for Teachers of RE (EFTRE) where a brief article is available via the "RE Across Europe" interactive map: http://www.eftre.net/. (Click on Northern Ireland on the map.)

Author's acknowledgements

Author's acknowledgements
I am grateful to all those who have helped and inspired me to shape
and develop these thoughts, and particularly to the following: my
colleague, James Nelson, as mentioned above; teachers from a wide
range of schools and many student teachers with whom I have
worked; the Revd Dr Roger Purce, Secretary of Christian Education
Movement Northern Ireland, for his own work in promoting mutual
understanding through RE-related activities and for his support and
endorsement for this project; Lat Blaylock of RE Today Services and
NATRE, for his support and encouragement; Professor Cornelia Roux
of North-West University, South Africa, for her help with updating
the short section on RE in post-apartheid South Africa; Marit Svare
for her helpful update on RE in Norway; Zoë Keens, Anstice Hughes
and their editorial colleagues at Christian Education/RE Today for
their support and creativity in bringing this project to fruition; Ray
Mullan and colleagues at the Northern Ireland Community Relations
Council for their generous support and encouragement in the
production of this book; my colleague, Richard Greenwood, for his
photography, including the cover photograph; and to others who gave
significant assistance with the provision of photographs – Neville
Watson and David Thompson of Forge Integrated Primary School,
Belfast; Jane Karney and Gerry McVeigh, principals of Dunmurry
and St Colman's Primary Schools respectively; Jill Caskey of Northern
Ireland Children's Enterprise (NICE); Eamon McClean of the Speedwell
Trust; and to all others who kindly gave permission for the use
of photographs.

1 Some concerns about Religious Education

Religious Education may easily become part of the process of initiation into the tribalism of Northern Ireland.
John Greer and Eugene McElhinney: *Irish Christianity: A Guide for Teachers*, (Gill and Macmillan 1985)

The group accepted that religion was one of the darkest regions in education. The curriculum certainly needed to be developed in that area.
Maurna Crozier (ed) Report from Education Seminar Group, in *Cultural Traditions in Northern Ireland – Varieties of Irishness* (Queens University Belfast 1989)

Religious Education (RE) in schools is a contentious area. Some people dispute its right to a place in publicly funded schools because it is perceived to be about promoting a particular religious viewpoint. At the other end of the spectrum, some people unashamedly argue for RE in schools as a way of promoting religious faith (sometimes termed 'confessional' teaching), claiming support from an apparent majority of parents and even sometimes from Human Rights documents.[2] Sometimes these positions are perceived to be the only options – a simplistic 'all-or-nothing' assumption in which RE is presumed to be supported by religious people and rejected by those who are not religious.

---

2   Some Human Rights statements affirm the right of children to be educated in the religion of their parents – as for instance in Article 5 of the 1981 *UN Declaration on the Elimination of All Forms of Intolerance and Discrimination Based on Religion or Belief*. Such statements, however, surely need to be balanced against other human rights principles which emphasise the importance of children valuing not just their own but other cultures also, and of developing tolerance and respect for all human beings (as in the Final Document of the *UN International Consultative Conference on School Education in Religion with Freedom of Religion and Belief* (2001). See Appendix 3 on Education and religion: perspectives from human rights (p54).

Here, however, a case will be made for Religious Education from an open, inclusive and non-confessional position, suggesting that it merits consideration as an important aspect of human experience and as an *antidote* to any attempts at religious indoctrination – which is a view that can also be supported by recourse to the views of parents and, indeed, human rights documents. It is from this position that the view is taken by this author that RE in schools can, and indeed should, be a shared educational enterprise, capable of being taught to pupils of all religious and cultural backgrounds together in any type of school, no less than any other area of the curriculum.

Public perceptions of Religious Education

Before considering in detail the possibilities of an inclusive approach to Religious Education, it may be helpful to outline some of the issues in the discussion about the place of religious education in a culturally and religiously plural society. One of the greatest difficulties lies in the persistent public perception that religious education is about promoting a particular religious view of life, whether this be a specific denominational position as in the case of church schools or a non-denominational position, as in the case of the state-controlled schools in Northern Ireland. It does not seem to have occurred to many people that RE can be taught in a more open way, and so a confessional purpose for RE is often simply assumed as the norm – in many cases probably reflecting what people remember from when they were at school.

This presumption that schools (and therefore the religion that is taught in them) have an inevitable religious/denominational bias is confirmed in many people's minds by the fact that Catholic maintained schools in Northern Ireland receive 100 per cent government funding, and by the existence of significant funding for other voluntary denominationally managed schools. The impression is further compounded by the continuation of conscience clauses which permit parents to request the withdrawal of their children from RE classes, the right on the part of teachers to request not to teach RE and the fact that in most schools RE is supposed to be inspected by the clergy rather than regular schools inspectors from the Education and Training Inspectorate. If RE really is open and free from pressure, and if it is as fully educational as any other subject in the curriculum, so the argument goes, why is there a need to 'protect' it with these conscience clauses and to deny teachers the right of inspection from within their own profession?[3]

The role of the Christian Churches

In many countries in Europe, RE has traditionally been defined and managed by the Churches or other religious groups. Some states have moved away from this position to a more inclusive approach, for example where a wide range of religious communities have a say, along with other interest groups, in planning RE syllabuses. Elsewhere, however, RE continues to be treated as a faith-based or confessional subject with the express purpose of promoting or nurturing religious faith. This has sometimes been done in a spirit of openness and generosity towards minority faith communities, but all too often it has been in a mood of defensiveness whereby denominational or other religious privilege in relation to RE has been firmly retained.

The significant role of the four largest Christian denominations in Northern Ireland in having been given responsibility by the Department of Education for devising a Core Syllabus for Religious Education, without any involvement by members of other faith communities, further serves to convince many people that RE is indeed a confessional subject. All other subjects in the Northern Ireland Curriculum are developed and reviewed by government-appointed public working parties, whereas RE sits outside this arrangement. Although grant-aided schools are legally required to provide RE, it is not listed as one of the 'Areas of Learning and Contributory Elements' of the Northern Ireland Curriculum.[4] The Churches' Core Syllabus that

---

3   The issue of withdrawal from RE is dealt with on pp43–4.
4   These 'Areas of Learning and Contributory Elements' are listed in Schedule 1 of the Education (Northern Ireland) Order 2006 (http://www.legislation.gov.uk/nisi/2006/1915/schedule/1). Since 1989, successive education legislation in Northern Ireland has specified that a 'Core Syllabus for Religious Education' should be devised by 'persons having an interest in the teaching of RE in grant-aided schools'. The Department of Education, however, has consistently granted this role to the four largest Christian denominations: the Catholic Church in Ireland; the Presbyterian Church in Ireland; the Church of Ireland; and the Methodist Church in Ireland.

first came into operation in 1993 was exclusively Christian in tone and content, and despite the inclusion in the Revised Core Syllabus (from September 2007) of some limited teaching of other religions at Key Stage 3 only, the rationale, content and ethos of the Northern Ireland Core Syllabus for RE remain unambiguously Christian, based on an argument that Northern Ireland 'is still a Christian country' and that primary school children will be confused by studying 'other religions' (Churches' Working Party 2003).

For many years, following the issuing of the original Core Syllabus, even pupils taking the Northern Ireland GCSE in Religious Studies did not have an opportunity of studying world faiths other than Christianity, though this possibility is now gradually being reinstated. In the Northern Ireland A-level syllabus the only world religions option is a study of Islam but, unsurprisingly in view of these limitations, this is taken up only by a small number of schools. These very narrow confines around RE in Northern Ireland simply confirm many people's worst fears about the nature of the subject.

The legal right of clergy to inspect RE instead of the Northern Ireland Education and Training Inspectorate (who may only inspect RE if specifically requested by a Board of Governors – which is quite rare) creates further difficulties. This right of clergy may well add to the perception that RE is little more than an arm of the Christian Churches. The fact, however, that relatively few clergy these days make a formal inspection of RE, quite probably out of sensitivity towards the professionalism of teachers, only adds to the problems, especially in many controlled and integrated schools because there is therefore no mechanism for any kind of professional quality control in relation to the teaching of RE.

Evaluating outcomes and experiences of RE

In my work with student teachers, including those specialising in Religious Studies, I find myself in a position to evaluate how some young adults have experienced their 14 years of school-based RE. Some have clearly valued their experience, but many are critical of it, and both kinds of experiences seem to have motivated those who wish to become specialist teachers of RE themselves. Specialists aside, there often appears to be a good deal of cynicism and not a little indifference to the subject, and these negatives are sometimes confirmed by what students experience in their school placements.

Some of the 'outcomes of RE' that I encounter, within and outside the teaching profession, give me particular cause for concern. Chief among these is the lack of awareness of religious diversity, both in relation to Christianity and other religions, and the unwillingness of many people to discuss it, especially in what they perceive as 'mixed' company. Despite years of classroom RE, the majority of students readily acknowledge their relatively sheltered experience and a lack of awareness of religious traditions other than their own; all but a few have never studied any religion other than Christianity. In some young adults this may express itself in defensiveness and occasionally even a self-assured arrogance, leading to a readiness to dismiss other people's faiths. Studies of Northern Ireland student teacher attitudes towards religious diversity (Richardson 2003a; 2006), however, indicated that many of them, from both Catholic and Protestant backgrounds, are very open to increasing their experience of religious diversity, albeit with an awareness of how they have been thwarted by lack of opportunity.

Another 'outcome' which causes concern is the far too common myth that any discussion of religious issues, especially in the presence of people from a different religious tradition, is likely to cause offence. This appears to deflect many teachers from consideration of differing beliefs for fear of provoking religious conflict in the classroom or of upsetting parents or members of the clergy. If such openness about religion has never been part of a teacher's own experience, as a pupil or as a student or in their personal activities, this reluctance to discuss religious issues on an equal basis is likely, quite understandably, to be reinforced.

RE and religious minorities

If the narrowness of the curriculum disadvantages children and young people from Catholic or Protestant backgrounds by limiting their awareness of diversity within Christianity, it also creates problems for families from minority faith communities. Research (Richardson

2003b) was carried out with parents from minority faiths who had children at school in Northern Ireland, including members of the Muslim, Hindu, Bahá'í, Jewish, Buddhist and Sikh communities, plus a few parents with no religious involvement. Only a small number of these parents indicated that RE in their child's school ever included consideration of their own religions and beliefs, or indeed of any religion other than Christianity. Most of those who indicated that there was some broader teaching indicated that it was 'very little', or used the word 'occasionally'.

When asked about the extent to which they were satisfied with the RE provided by their child's school, two-thirds indicated that they were 'dissatisfied' or 'very dissatisfied', and about half of the remainder indicated that they were 'unsure'. One Hindu parent indicated amazement that Northern Ireland was 'so far behind' compared with her own experience of religious education 30 years earlier in England. A very large majority agreed or agreed strongly that they would like more consideration of their own religious faith in school RE classes, and an even larger majority wanted their children to learn about a range of different religions in RE.

The parents were strongly in favour of the provision of better information and training for teachers in relation to minority faith concerns, and particularly in relation to how to deal with prejudice and racism. The great majority of them supported the provision of RE, but suggested that it must be a changed, fair and balanced provision if they are to feel heard and respected.

Several later studies (Mawhinney 2006; 2007; Mawhinney *et al* 2010) have reflected similar concerns on the part of parents and/ or children from minority belief backgrounds (including people who are not religious) about the confessional or doctrinal nature of RE in many primary and post-primary schools. One parent, commenting on the RE that his child had received in a post-primary school, observed that 'I expected [RE] to be much more valuing of different religions, religious backgrounds and of humanists or people of no religion but I haven't found any of that. I have found it very dogmatic' (Mawhinney *et al* 2010).

In these studies a majority of respondents indicated that they were not opposed to RE as such, but that they wanted it to be more broadly based and inclusive of other world religions as well as Christianity.

Teachers' reluctance

Anxieties are sometimes articulated by serving teachers which amount to a reluctance to deviate from traditional approaches to RE or to get involved with issues of religious diversity. Among non-specialist teachers, such concerns may focus on feeling out of their depth in relation to opening up religious topics, influenced by a culture that often avoids such issues out of fear of causing offence. Some teachers take refuge in a cocoon of reinforced ignorance, arguing that their own lack of knowledge is reason enough not to explore diversity. Wariness of relativism or syncretism may sometimes be expressed as the reason for not dealing with issues of diverse religious experience. Sometimes it is suggested that only a convinced believer in a particular tradition or religion has the capacity and right to teach that religion, or that teaching by someone outside a particular faith tradition would inevitably be superficial.

Even in schools where there is a strong commitment to teaching Catholics and Protestants together, similar concerns can be evident. A survey of RE in 20 integrated primary schools carried out by members of the Northern Ireland Council for Integrated Education's RE Focus Group (NICIE 2002) made it clear that most teachers in the survey seemed wary of straying from what they perceived to be the 'norms' of RE as they have known them – that is, adopting the generally biblical approach found in most controlled schools (those catering mainly for the Protestant community) plus the provision of sacramental teaching for Catholic pupils. The survey results indicated very few attempts at that time to deal with the issues of religious diversity at any level. Constraints seemed to stem from lack of time, lack of awareness or training in diversity issues and, perhaps understandably, a preoccupation on the part of many integrated primary schools with the issue of provision for Catholic pupils in relation to preparation for the sacraments.

Observations made by student teachers on primary school placements in controlled and integrated schools (Richardson 2008) were mainly a record of their disappointment at the discovery of poor-quality approaches to RE in many schools. Students drew attention to the frequent practice of class teachers avoiding having to teach RE by swapping subjects with another teacher. Many noted that pedagogical approaches were very unimaginative – often a worksheet-based approach using cloze procedures and word searches, for example – and that there were limited opportunities for pupils to share in discussion. In some schools RE appeared to be un-coordinated or even completely neglected, and some teachers openly admitted that their classes did not do RE (made possible by the absence of a proper inspection regime for RE). A few student teachers expressed concerns about class teachers who appeared to be using RE as a form of proselytisation (and this has also sometimes been noted by students reflecting on their own post-primary school experience).

The lack of any teaching on religious diversity issues ('to avoid offending anyone') was of particular concern to some of the students. Some of those who had been on placement in integrated schools noted that some teachers sought to avoid anything religiously controversial by focusing their 'RE' only on moral education. Another concern noted by some students placed in integrated primary schools was that RE appeared to be the only subject for which Catholic and Protestant pupils were actually sometimes (or even always) separated – quite contrary to what they had expected in such schools.[5]

Despite some changes to the Core Syllabus to include world religions and more specific teaching about Catholic and Protestant traditions at Key Stage 3, evidence continues to suggest that reluctance to engage with RE can be found among many teachers in different types of schools. Some specialist RE teachers in post-primary schools clearly welcomed the opportunity to teach a broader

---

5   Integrated primary schools in particular have understandably tried to ensure that Catholic families would not feel disadvantaged by sending their children to integrated schools and so have sought to reassure parents by making provision for sacramental preparation as would be given in Catholic primary schools. This, however, creates the dilemma of separation, a concern with which many teachers in integrated primary schools continue to struggle.

curriculum while others seemed to find the inclusion of world religions more challenging, at least initially.

Opportunities to teach awareness and understanding across the Catholic and Protestant divide are made significantly difficult by the persistent separateness of educational provision in the great majority of schools, whereby over 90 per cent of pupils continue to attend schools which are perceived to serve 'their own religious/cultural community'. The lack of opportunity for regular interpersonal cross-community encounter does not much help the process of education for mutual understanding. Many of these concerns in post-primary schools are compounded by the pressures on timetabling which often leave RE 'squeezed' and marginalised despite the best efforts of committed teachers, and there are still too many schools where the use of non-specialist teachers to fill gaps in the timetable creates additional difficulties.

A more recent survey of teachers in controlled, maintained and integrated primary schools (Richardson 2012), however, while reflecting a range of views including some of those outlined above, actually indicated a growing level of readiness to deal more openly with issues of religious diversity – including similarities and differences between Catholics and Protestants as well as between different world religions. Similarly, post-primary specialist RE teachers appear to have grown in confidence over recent years in approaching diversity-related themes. Nevertheless, it is clear that there is a long way to go in the process of developing teachers' capacity and confidence to deal with a breadth of religious issues in schools, and this has significant implications for teacher education at all levels.

Religious Education for openness

Despite all the difficulties and disadvantages indicated above, it is possible to take a positive view of the educational potential of RE. Educators who are prepared to work through these difficulties agree that RE is a subject with great possibilities, not least in challenging ignorance with increased understanding. Well-taught RE can provide an excellent medium for exploring the similarities and differences between different forms of Christianity, especially in a society where many Catholics and Protestants still have little or no opportunity for interpersonal encounter. In a society that is becoming increasingly globally aware and ethnically and culturally diverse, thoughtful RE can open up perceptions and experiences and enable encounters with unfamiliar religious traditions and with secular beliefs.

Some critics of RE in the past have accused the subject of being an attempt to indoctrinate children. Such an accusation needs careful examination, but it is perhaps not surprising in those contexts where one form of religion is promoted as something that children 'ought to believe' or where one view is taught to the exclusion of others. Yet far from being an agent of closing minds, soundly taught educational RE can be an opener of minds and a challenger of prejudice – a process that the writer David Hay has described as *de-indoctrination*:

> *Religious educators are sometimes accused of attempting to indoctrinate their pupils. But when religious education is correctly understood, it becomes clear that it is the reverse of indoctrination. What it does is to demonstrate that there is more than one perspective on reality. It enlarges, rather than diminishes, freedom.*
> **(Hay 1990: 15)**

The best way to counter prejudice and indoctrination, one might argue, is through those very aspects of education where there might appear to be the greatest danger of them occurring. To *avoid* teaching such a controversial subject is to give credence to the argument that it is not possible to do so in an open and fair manner. In other words, if we want to counter religious exclusivism and open people's minds to unfamiliar ideas and situations, well-taught RE is crucial, especially in situations where there is a 'given' diversity – such as in the classrooms of shared or integrated schools, or, indeed, in a growing number of controlled and maintained schools around an increasingly plural Northern Ireland.

2 Religious Education: reflections and challenges

Competence Statement No.8: Teachers will have developed a knowledge and understanding of the need to take account of the significant features of pupils' cultures, languages and faiths and to address the implications for learning arising from these.
from *Teaching: The Reflective Profession*, General Teaching Council for Northern Ireland 2007

The main focus of this section will be to reflect on the most appropriate purposes of, and approaches to, Religious Education in Northern Ireland. In a society that is religiously and culturally divided and increasingly diverse, what are the key elements that must be included, and how can the curriculum be appropriately balanced in a way that meets the needs of children from all these backgrounds? In particular how can this be done in a culturally/religiously mixed school – integrated, shared or whatever else it may be called – and what structures and support will best facilitate that process? Is there, indeed, a case for an RE Syllabus that is specifically designed for integrated or collaborating schools and that could perhaps be used by others who wish to begin to take a more inclusive approach?

Differences do matter!

A view is sometimes articulated by those who wish to take a moderate position in relation to religious diversity that 'differences don't matter' because 'we're all the same really'! While such a view may sometimes stem from a genuine recognition of the large areas of commonality between, for example, Catholic and Protestant Christians or even between Christianity and other faiths, it can be dangerous and counterproductive because it tends to play down the real and significant differences between people from different religious and cultural backgrounds for the sake of a simplistic unity. This position, which at an extreme becomes dishonest, should surely also be regarded as an undesirable outcome of RE, particularly if it occurs in a setting where there are real opportunities to explore diversity first-hand.

The reality is that there *are* real and significant differences, within as well as between religions. Religions make truth claims which often conflict with other truth claims, and we do no justice to religious understanding and dialogue if we try to diminish them or to play them down. Some writers on religious education have given considerable emphasis to this point and teachers must also be realistic and honest about it. In acknowledging such differences we can engage in a process that involves a willingness to listen, to share ideas, to understand and to develop respect. A key dimension of RE teaching is the capacity to model honest and respectful approaches to dealing with difference.

Constraints and options in RE

A case is sometimes made for the complete removal of religion from schools in favour of a secular approach to education, as has been the case in some countries for many years; France, the United States and some former Soviet Bloc countries are often cited as examples of this, though the reasons in each case are significantly different. The argument that there should be no religious teaching or religious worship in publicly funded schools may well seem an attractive and highly desirable option for families who are not religious and sometimes perhaps also to those who belong to small religious minorities.

In Northern Ireland there is evidence that some parents may have initially chosen integrated schools because they wanted a secular option – 'to get away from Protestant or Catholic schools' – only to find to their surprise that integrated schools often have to make additional religious provision in order to justify their inclusive status. This desire may well be based on the persistent assumption that if schools are teaching religion it means that they are actually *promoting* religious faith – which may well be based on real past personal experience for some people. A key purpose of this document, however, is to suggest that this is not – or should not – be the purpose of RE and that the basis of any religious teaching must be thoroughly educational.

I have already argued that there is a positive case for including RE in the school curriculum in all kinds of schools, despite my many frustrations with the way in which it is presently officially framed and publicly perceived. A 'secular escape' from religion in schools does not do justice to the reality that children need to have an understanding of their encounters with religion as a significant dimension of human experience – its various expressions, its language, its thought, its concerns, its impact on people's feelings – if they are to have a rounded and balanced view of the contemporary world. The ways in which religion is currently taught in schools may well require considerable review, but its place and significance within a soundly educational framework should not be in doubt.

The challenge

Despite these difficulties and obstacles I believe that RE has a very important role to play in the development of shared education in Northern Ireland. In order to take a more positive direction, however, it will be necessary to move away unambiguously from the traditional perception of RE as the promotion of religious belief. The alternative, genuinely educational, approach is surely about developing religious awareness and understanding in an inclusive manner, appropriate to a culturally and religiously plural society. Good-quality open RE can challenge attitudes and stereotypes and make people think; in promoting dialogue it offers an alternative to oppositional authoritarian monologues; in building relationships it can help to counter prejudice, suspicion and fear.

The challenge of RE in schools in a divided and diverse society is not to find ways of avoiding it so as to prevent it from becoming a nasty and divisive issue in the classroom, but rather of finding ways of making RE work positively for understanding and improved relationships. This will require a change from the current Churches-dominated system, which will undoubtedly be a difficult transition. It does not mean that there would be no role for the Churches, but rather that they along with others (other Christian traditions, other world religions and belief systems and non-religious groups such as Humanists) would need to work in partnership, as is the case in some other jurisdictions.

If the concept of 'sharing Religious Education' is to mean anything, the working partnership on which it is based will need to be broad and inclusive. The existence of separate schooling sectors, at least partly based on religious differences, certainly makes this more difficult to achieve, as genuine sharing requires that people encounter each other and do things together. Northern Ireland's separate systems are likely to continue for some time, but as sharing between those sectors is increasingly encouraged and tried, it will be important to ensure that RE is not left out and that *sharing RE* becomes a genuine part of that process.[6]

The perception that teaching RE to people of different religions together is too difficult and potentially offensive remains strong in some quarters. The non-denominational teacher education institution where I work has traditionally catered primarily for students from a Protestant community background, but in recent years has become considerably more 'mixed'. One of the most rewarding aspects of my work there has been to observe this change and to have the opportunity of teaching Religious Studies to Catholics and Protestants together in the process of preparing them to teach RE in different kinds of schools. The attitude of some former colleagues was to counsel extreme caution 'for fear of offence', but the actual experience has been very different – a very positive and creative opportunity for sharing, dialogue and mutual understanding. Religious diversity in any classroom can and should be an open door leading to greater awareness and empathetic understanding.

In a rare review in 2000 of Religious Education in the Province's schools, the Northern Ireland Education and Training Inspectorate commented favourably on the importance of a broadly based approach to RE:

A study of the various Christian denominations and other,
world, religions within Northern Ireland, at a level appropriate

---

6   The issue of RE in church/faith schools is dealt with later in this document in the section on 'Confessional teaching' (p41–3).

to the age and ability of the pupils, acknowledges the increasingly pluralistic nature of modern society ... Furthermore [it] can deepen and broaden the pupils' understanding of their own faith, can make a valuable contribution to developing tolerance and can support the aims of the educational themes of Education for Mutual Understanding and Cultural Heritage. **(ETI 2000:1)**[7]

---

7   At the time of this ETI report, 'Education for Mutual Understanding' (EMU) and 'Cultural Heritage' were statutory cross-curricular themes in the Northern Ireland Curriculum. Since 2007 they have been redeveloped into 'Personal Development and Mutual Understanding' (PDMU – for primary schools) and 'Local and Global Citizenship' (for post-primary schools).

3 Inclusive Religious Education

The organisation of the curriculum for RE can be considered good when ... all pupils, regardless of gender, ability or religious belief, experience a programme which is sensitive to the diversity of religious and cultural experience within the school and wider community.
Education and Training Inspectorate, *Evaluating Religious Education* (ETI 2000)

The key argument presented here is that inclusive and open-ended approaches to understanding religion are highly desirable in any society that wishes to move from religiously related conflict towards mutual understanding and respect – and they are essential for schools of any type that wish to engage in greater sharing across traditional boundaries. This kind of approach to RE has to be built up, of course, and there are some key building-blocks in the process, the most important of which are:

- an inclusive and safe ethos
- an open educational rationale for RE
- a balanced RE curriculum.

An inclusive and safe ethos
In schools where there is a genuine diversity of cultural backgrounds and religious commitments (including children from families where there is no religious involvement) RE has tremendous potential as one of the key formative subjects which can be used to develop new ways of learning to value and respect difference. This is a counter-statement to the familiar playing-it-safe view that 'we don't speak about differences here'! It is a statement that real open sharing is both desirable and possible and much more constructive than silence and avoidance. I am reminded of the poster that I used to have in my classroom, of an old sailing ship with the slogan: 'A ship in a harbour

is safe – but that is not what ships are for!' To extend the metaphor, we need to 'push the boat out' and learn how to sail it.

If such sharing is to happen, however, we have to create a safe and secure space for all members of the school – children, teachers, ancillary staff and parents – to support each other in this openness. This is a task that goes beyond just the subject of RE: it is dependent upon a positive whole-school ethos, within which the acknowledgement of, and respect for, diversity is a central precept. Adults within such an environment have a particularly important role in modelling this open and positive approach to religious and cultural diversity.

Some teachers in integrated schools or other shared situations have occasionally expressed their genuine concern that if they start to talk openly about sensitive issues they will spoil the good relationships that have been built up between colleagues from different backgrounds. This is understandable, but it is an anxiety which has to be recognised and then worked through if real progress is to be made. One of the key factors in this whole process will be teachers' capacity to talk and discuss openly and comfortably among themselves about religion and religious issues, modelling the behaviour that they desire for their pupils and thereby giving permission for pupils also to talk about religion and difference. Such approaches require careful leadership, and headteachers must make adequate time for them to be addressed in staff development programmes. In some schools, staff development sessions have been specifically allocated so that teachers can spend time together in order to work at these crucial issues of developing an inclusive ethos and safe space (see Murray 2010).

An open educational rationale for RE

Religious Education that is focused on developing open appreciation for diversity needs to have clearly *educational* aims. Aims that are only specific to committed members of one religious community (whether this is defined as Catholic, Protestant or just simply Christian or any other faith) are fundamentally confessional and inappropriate to the broad educational needs of children from a diversity of backgrounds. (The possible place for confessional or doctrinal teaching in schools – such as preparing children for the sacraments in Catholic schools – is discussed on p41).

Such a set of overall aims for Religious Education, as a basis for shared, inclusive teaching, might look something like the points laid out in Box 1. Any set of educational aims will have to be adapted to the age and developmental level of the learners, of course.

Box 1: Religious Education seeks, over time, to help children and young people ...

- to explore and understand religion in its various expressions
- to develop an awareness of the language and practice of various religions
- to explore the links between religious belief, ethical/moral issues and shared human values with awareness and understanding
- to understand how religion can be a powerful influence, positively or negatively, on people's lives, individually and in communities
- to value and respect religious diversity and to learn how to live with it in a shared society
- to be aware of the importance of feelings and emotions in relation to religious matters
- to develop skills in discussing and reflecting on religious and ethical/moral issues with criticality and maturity
- to develop a sensitive awareness of various approaches to spirituality and provide opportunities for spiritual development
- to develop an open-ended basis for their own religious and ethical choices
- to engage in responsible religious dialogue which involves the right to a voice and the responsibility to listen.

The broadly based aims proposed in Box 1 might be used to provide a stimulus for discussion among teachers as to what is appropriate in their particular school. A statement of purposes for RE should ideally be agreed and owned by those who will teach it. This will be particularly important where teachers are used to a more confessional or denominational approach to RE, or where a mono-faith approach has traditionally been assumed.

A balanced RE curriculum – options and models

A significant weakness of traditional approaches to RE in many schools in Northern Ireland has been that they have provided only what I would term *Christian education*, rather than Religious Education in a fuller sense. In Catholic schools this has been quite consciously based around 'faith formation' – nurturing children in the Catholic faith that they are assumed already to be following. In controlled schools, mainly serving children from an assumed Protestant background (some would say 'culturally Protestant'), this has legally been 'non-denominational' but still significantly Christian in its assumptions and content. There are currently no faith schools serving Jews, Muslims or other religious communities in Northern Ireland, though this has sometimes been hinted at, with occasional requests by such communities for opportunities for instruction in their own faiths.

RE is widely perceived as Christian RE, a perception that is reinforced by the absence of teaching about world religions in most primary schools and even, until very recently, in post-primary schools. These distinct and separate approaches to RE are potentially disruptive to the concept of a common curriculum experience and run the risk, in an already divided and diverse society, of contributing to ignorant, hostile and sectarian attitudes towards 'the other', not least if separate RE is carried even into schools which are otherwise shared or integrated.

Religious Education in a growing range of countries, however, has moved away from a traditionally confessional approach to a much more balanced and inclusive position, and a glance at these may serve as useful models for those societies which are still in the process of reflection and change. In this regard the syllabuses, structures and processes of development in England, Scotland, Norway and South Africa are worth particular examination.

Religious Education in **England** was traditionally focused on the Bible and Christianity until the 1960s, but has undergone many changes since then, significantly in response to the increasingly plural and multi-religious nature of British society. Multifaith approaches to teaching religion have been prominent since the mid-1970s and, under the present arrangements, Religious Education is planned co-operatively by a body in each educational administrative area known as the Standing Advisory Council on Religious Education (SACRE) in which there is significant partnership between representatives of the different faith communities.

Non-statutory advice and guidelines were previously produced by government, including the production in the 1990s of model syllabuses which emphasised the importance in RE of 'learning *about* religion' and 'learning *from* religion'. A *Non-Statutory National Framework for Religious Education* was developed (QCA 2004), emphasising the importance in RE of learning from 'different religions, beliefs, values and traditions while exploring their own beliefs and questions of meaning'. This document challenged pupils 'to reflect on, consider, analyse, interpret and evaluate issues of truth, belief, faith and ethics', emphasising the importance of pupils developing 'their sense of identity and belonging' and flourishing 'individually within their communities and as citizens in a pluralistic society and global community'.

In 2013 the Religious Education Council for England and Wales, which draws together a wide range of interested parties (including professional bodies, many different faith communities, humanists and others) in order to keep a watching brief on the overall development of the subject, issued a Review of Religious Education in England, suggesting that the overall aims of the subject should be to ensure that all pupils:

- know about and understand a range of religions and worldviews;
- express ideas and insights about the nature, significance and impact of religions and worldviews; and

- gain and deploy the skills needed to engage seriously with religions and worldviews (REC 2013: 14-15).

The subject Religious and Moral Education (RME) in **Scotland** is a statutory core subject for all pupils and 'includes learning about Christianity, Islam and other world religions, and supports the development of beliefs and values' (http://www.educationscotland.gov.uk/). According to official documentation following revisions to the curriculum in 2011:

> *Through their learning in religious and moral education all children and young people will develop an understanding of Christianity, which has shaped the history and traditions of Scotland and continues to exert an influence on national life. It is also a fundamental principle that all children and young people throughout Scotland will consider a range of faiths and views, whatever their own situation and local context.*
> **(Curriculum for Excellence Scotland, n.d.)**

The Scottish approach emphasises the importance of the development of the whole person in terms of self-awareness and awareness of others (often termed 'personal search') and the development of respect in the context of a plural society.

In **Norway** the previous traditional Christian syllabus was replaced in 1997 by a subject known originally as 'Christianity, Religion, Life Stances' but changed again in 2008 (after a dispute and ruling by the European Court of Human Rights) to 'Religion, Philosophies of Life and Ethics'. It is non-confessional and multifaith, and is designed to be 'an ordinary school subject intended to bring all pupils together'. The key areas for study are Christianity (including its significance in Norwegian cultural heritage), other world religions and philosophies, and ethical and philosophical themes. Pupils are encouraged to learn to talk with those who have different religious and philosophical views, in a spirit of 'respect for religious values, human rights in general and the ethical foundation of all human rights', in order to gain 'ethical awareness and understanding across religious faiths and cultural borders' (Norwegian Directorate for Education and Training, n.d.).

Developments in Religious Education in post-apartheid **South Africa** (1994) also provide an interesting point of comparison for those considering options in Northern Ireland. During the apartheid years the 'single faith approach' to teaching religion in schools (Christian National Education) had been based on the simplistic assumption that South Africa was a Christian country. The initial post-apartheid alternative was to initiate a 'multiple-single tradition' approach with RE being taken separately according to the faith community to which children belonged, but there were many concerns expressed that this would simply create a form of religious apartheid, accompanied by mutual ignorance and mistrust.

With the publication of the South African Department of Education's *Policy on Religion and Education* (2003), a co-operative model to religious education was adopted. The approach is multi-religious, irrespective of the religious and/or cultural ethos of the school, and led to the present 'Religion Education' programme which, in the words of the South African Department of Education: 'contributes to the wider framework of education by developing in every learner the knowledge, values attitudes and skills necessary for diverse religions to co-exist in a multi-religious society' (quoted in Chidester 2003).

These examples may not be perfect models of how RE might be re-shaped in Northern Ireland, but they do offer perspectives on alternative ways forward which can be helpful in considering future options. They contribute weight to the case for an approach to RE that recognises and responds positively to the realities of a diverse society.

International standards

Alongside these processes of change in individual countries there has been significant international interest in how religion is dealt with in schools, almost certainly reflecting concerns following the 9/11 attacks on the United States and other incidents in which religious extremism is perceived to have played an important role. Conferences, discussions and statements have been forthcoming from many bodies, including the United Nations and UNESCO, relating to the importance of religious awareness and understanding in the process of education about democracy and human rights. A United Nations Consultative Conference on Education and the Freedom of Religion and Belief in 2001 declared that 'education, in particular at school, should contribute in a meaningful way to promote tolerance and respect for the freedom of religion and belief'. Amongst its recommendations it proposed that schools should 'promote and respect educational policies aimed at strengthening the promotion of human rights and the eradication of prejudices, and ensuring respect for and acceptance of pluralism and diversity in the field of religion and belief', and that 'teachers and students should be provided with voluntary opportunities for meetings and exchanges with their counterparts of different religions or beliefs' (United Nations 2001b).

Particular interest in this issue has been taken by the Council of Europe, and reference has been made to the importance of RE as a dimension of intercultural education in various documents over recent years. Notably this was highlighted in the Council's White Paper on Intercultural Dialogue, *Living Together as Equals in Dignity*, which promotes 'knowledge and understanding of the major world religions and non-religious convictions' as an important dimension of what it terms 'the learning and teaching of intercultural competences' (CoE 2008a: 42-43). An excellent handbook for teachers was also produced by the Council, including many practical case studies from around Europe: *Religious Diversity and Intercultural Education: A Reference Book for Schools*, edited by John Keast (2007) who currently serves as the Chair of the RE Council for England and Wales.

In an attempt to offer internationally acceptable standards relating to the teaching of religious issues in public schools, another international body, the Office for Democratic Institutions and Human Rights (ODIHR) of the Organisation for Security and Co-operation in Europe (OSCE), issued the *Toledo Guiding Principles on Teaching about Religions and Beliefs in Public Schools* (OSCE/ODIHR 2007), based on the work of an international advisory council of lawyers, educationists and human rights experts. The document makes many valuable suggestions and includes a set of 'Key Guiding Principles', with an emphasis on inclusion, balance, fairness, mutual respect and the sound professional preparation of teachers.[8]

Curriculum and balance in Northern Ireland

Changes to the RE curriculum in other countries, together with the growing interest in these matters on the part of international organisations, offer various pointers for the future of the subject in Northern Ireland.

In all types of schools, including those most committed to a 'faith formation' approach, there are challenges around the issues of diversity and inclusion in teaching RE that must be faced. Nevertheless it seems that in many schools in Northern Ireland relatively little thought has been given to this, despite some notable exceptions. In many areas the view that 'it's not an issue here' can still be heard, although this is a hollow argument in the light of the significant exposure that children and young people have to religious, ethnic and cultural diversity through television, the internet and other media, whether or not they are sharing a classroom with children from diverse backgrounds. It could indeed be argued that children in schools that are least affected by diversity – whether this be in relation to Catholics and Protestants or a wider range of differing ethnic, cultural and religious groups – are perhaps *most* in need of an approach to RE that takes cultural diversity and inclusion seriously.

This issue is perhaps particularly significant for teachers and pupils in schools where there is an existing commitment to integration or cross-community sharing and to inclusive education in general. Yet despite some consideration having been given to the issue by various schools or groups of teachers over the years, the evidence suggests that there is no agreed approach to the provision of a balanced curriculum for Religious Education specifically for integrated schools or for other diverse educational environments.

Some have suggested that such a development would be highly desirable, but so far this goal has not been achieved. In fact, integrated schools have tended to give greater attention to meeting the needs of particular denominations – especially the catechetical expectations

8   For further details on international standards, see Appendix 3.

of many Catholic parents – and therefore focusing more on separate provision (although many of the schools also set out to teach at least some RE to all pupils together). Many integrated schools have used the RE programmes developed for Catholic schools – *Alive-O* in primary schools (with some adaptations for integrated school use), and the post-primary programme, *Fully Alive* – and there is certainly some broadly based material in these programmes which could be used much more widely than in the Catholic sector alone. Some parts of these programmes are very catechetical and confessional, however, and are therefore unsuitable for use as the total RE programme for the widest range of pupils. A programme entitled *Delving Deeper* (NICIE 2005) was developed by the Integrated Education Council for use by Protestant pupils in integrated primary schools while Catholics are taking part in sacramental preparation classes, but it is not clear how widely this has been used. It has been criticised for being overly representative of conservative evangelical Protestantism and it has also been pointed out that it does not solve the issue of provision for children from religions other than Christianity or those from families with no religious beliefs.

Some integrated schools have been much more adventurous in this area, however, and have developed their own schemes which have attempted to make their RE programme more inclusive and to organise their teaching in a way that does not emphasise separation. A NICIE publication designed to share more widely the experience of integrated schools, *ABC: Promoting an Anti-Bias Approach to Education in Northern Ireland* (2008), offers some valuable principles for an inclusive approach to religious, cultural and ethnic diversity and states that 'Religious education is a subject with great possibilities, not least in challenging ignorance with increased understanding' (p25). Yet despite what is surely great potential from within this sector to offer new models of RE appropriate for the religious pluralities of Northern Ireland, much of this potential so far remains untapped.

All grant-aided (publicly funded) schools in Northern Ireland are legally required to follow the Churches' Northern Ireland Core Syllabus for RE (in its revised form from September 2007), although the syllabus permits them, if they wish, to teach additional material 'beyond the core'. The reality for many teachers, however, is that they feel that there is too much already in the syllabus and that any suggestion of teaching additional material is out of the question. This Core Syllabus, the content of which has been devised by the four largest Christian denominations in Northern Ireland with Department of Education agreement, is unsurprisingly confessional in content and tone, despite being presented in a non-denominational manner. Although the Core Syllabus includes material which should quite reasonably form part of any RE programme, its greatest weakness is in its incompleteness and consequent narrowness.

The structure and 'Learning Objectives' of the 2007 Core Syllabus are shown in Figure 1 (p35). The wording of the three principal Learning Objectives is as given in the Core Syllabus documentation and apply from Foundation Stage to Key Stage 4; Learning Objective 3 applies to Key Stage 3 only.

Despite the fact that it was agreed by the numerically largest Christian denominations together (which many people hailed in the early 1990s as a significant ecumenical achievement), the syllabus seems simply to enshrine separate practice rather than encouraging greater sharing in the way that RE is taught. Its assumptions are exclusively Christian and somewhat narrowly conceived and, despite some of the high ideals on which it claims to be based, there is very little in it that helps teachers to deal with knowledge of and respect for diversity.

For example, one of the few actual references to diversity in the sections dealing with primary schools states that: 'Teachers should provide opportunities for pupils to … be aware of and have respect for differing cultures and faiths' (Core Syllabus, p19: Key Stage 2 – Morality (Department of Education NI 2007)) but no content or other guidance is offered that will help teachers to do this. For Key Stage 3 the 2007 Revised Syllabus included a new Learning Objective on World Religions (p29), and this has been welcomed in many quarters. Yet in their introductory document the Churches RE Review Working Party (2003) made the dismissive observation that the study of faiths other than Christianity 'will require only a modest amount of teaching time in each year of key stage 3' (p11).

Primary pupils explore
symbols and artefacts
from different faiths
© Richard Greenwood

Discovering Jewish
religious dress
© Richard Greenwood

(Top) 'Stained glass window' shared design by primary pupils | (Above) Primary pupils in an inter-school trust-building exercise designing 'stained glass windows'

(Top) A shared pulpit! © *The Speedwell Trust* | **(Above) Young people exploring religious traditions** © *NICE (Northern Ireland Children's Enterprise)*

Exploring religious diversity with puppets
© Richard Greenwood

Exploring Christian
artefacts from Catholic,
Protestant and
Orthodox traditions
© Richard Greenwood

**(Top) Primary pupils examine a Qur'an on a
Qur'an stand (rehal)** © *Richard Greenwood*
**| (Above) Young people exploring a church
together** © *NICE (Northern Ireland
Children's Enterprise)*

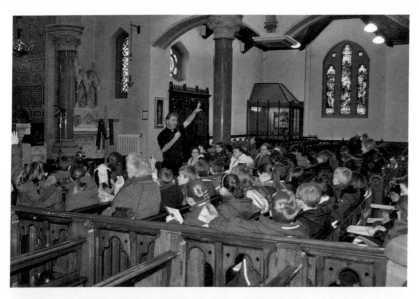

Children from different community backgrounds visit together
a Catholic church (above) and a Protestant church (below)
© *The Speedwell Trust*

Figure 1: Learning Objectives of the Northern Ireland Core Syllabus (2007 revision)

Learning Objective 1:
The Revelation of God
(all key stages)
Pupils should develop an awareness, knowledge, understanding and appreciation of the key Christian teachings about God (Father, Son and Holy Spirit), about Jesus Christ and about the Bible; and develop an ability to interpret and relate the Bible to life.

Learning Objective 2:
The Christian Church
(all key stages)
Pupils should develop a knowledge, understanding and appreciation of the growth of Christianity, of its worship, prayer and religious language; a growing awareness of the meaning of belonging to a Christian tradition; and sensitivity towards the beliefs of others.

Learning Objective 3:
Morality
(all key stages)
Pupils should develop their ability to think and judge about morality, to relate Christian moral principles to personal and social life, and to identify values and attitudes that influence behaviour.

Learning Objective 4:
World Religions
(Key Stage 3 only)
Pupils should be given an introduction to two world religions other than Christianity in order to develop knowledge of and sensitivity towards, the religious beliefs, practices and lifestyles of people from other religions in Northern Ireland.

The Core Syllabus in its original (1993) and revised (2007) forms was given the go-ahead by government despite considerable opposition from groups concerned with equality issues, inter-religious relations, human rights and community relations. Many people have argued that it runs counter to the requirements of equality legislation (most notably Section 75 of the Northern Ireland Act of 1998) and to the spirit of the government's policy statements in 'A Shared Future' (OFMDFM 2005) and later documents. At the time of writing there is no indication that the Department of Education and the Churches have any official plans to work towards a more intercultural and shared approach to RE, though there are some more hopeful signs that change is possible

Some teachers and schools at primary and post-primary levels have of late taken a much more robust approach to including religious diversity in their teaching programmes. Post-primary schools seem to have grown in confidence in relation to teaching the World Religions sections of the Revised Core Syllabus, despite continuing concerns about the lack of availability of professional development and support. Some primary teachers have shown a determination to include more religious-diversity-related topics in their teaching, perhaps helped by the introduction (since 2007) into the primary curriculum of Personal Development and Mutual Understanding (PDMU), which formally involves exploring similarities and differences and 'valuing and celebrating cultural difference and diversity' within its outline of minimum content. Surveys of student teachers and serving teachers (as indicated previously, pp8–9) have suggested that there is increased openness towards such inclusion, even if somewhat cautiously. The three primary Thematic Units,[9] published in 2010 by CCEA for the Religious Education Advisory Group (established after the 2007 Core Syllabus revision to provide support and guidance), include materials that go well beyond the confines of the content of the Core Syllabus, particularly in relation to Christian diversity and world religions at all key stages.

---

9   The three units are 'Food for Thought' (for Years 3 & 4), 'Saint Patrick and People of Faith' (for Year 5) and 'Faith and Light' (for Years 6 & 7). They are downloadable from the Northern Ireland Curriculum website: Key Stages 1 & 2, Religious Education.

These developments are encouraging, though many teachers still seem unwilling to go beyond the legal confines of the Core Syllabus. Until there are clear moves towards a more officially inclusive approach to RE, both in development and content, there will in my view be significant justification for educators and others who are committed to the principles of diversity and inclusion in Religious Education to continue to campaign for a much revised Core Syllabus. If we are to move forward in pursuing the aims of RE as suggested earlier in this section, then something more balanced and comprehensive will be required.

4 A model for inclusive Religious Education

Given the current constraints of the Northern Ireland Core Syllabus, what are the options for those who wish to teach Religious Education in an educational, balanced and inclusive manner that is suitable for *all* pupils together, whatever their cultural/religious background? A further revision of the RE Core Syllabus, based on experience from integrated or collaborating schools and an awareness of more intercultural models, would be a welcome development – but this may yet be some way off. So in the mean time some options are offered here for greater sharing and inclusivity in RE, based on awareness of effective practice locally and in other places.

In order to give some idea of what such a syllabus might look like, Figure 2 proposes a possible model and indicates some of the key areas that might be included. It was developed from earlier models which took shape over many years in the present author's classrooms and, later, in curriculum development work. In this format it was originally devised especially for a seminar in Bosnia-Herzegovina in 2001 in which the question was raised: *how can we teach religion positively and constructively in a religiously divided society?* It was further developed during and following a workshop held under the auspices of the Department of Education in the Republic of Georgia in 2004 which was also exploring these issues in relation to their own changing situation. Other modifications have continued to be made, including some based on the experience of working with other international groups around Europe.

Through its three strands (which bear some similarity to the main structure of the Northern Ireland Core Syllabus), this model recognises the religious traditions and communities present in a particular country or region, and gives due weight to the more prominent traditions while recognising the wider need for

Figure 2: Teaching religion educationally and inclusively: a balanced model for plural societies

In this balanced model it is assumed throughout that the syllabus will include:
• the religious tradition(s) or faith(s) that are familiar in a particular society
• other traditions/faiths/life-stances, including those which do not have a local presence.

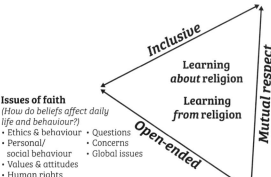

Sources of faith
(What do people believe?)
• Holy books
• Founders
• Characters
• Beliefs/ creeds
• Stories
• Teachings

Inclusive

Learning *about* religion

Learning *from* religion

Mutual respect

Issues of faith
(How do beliefs affect daily life and behaviour?)
• Ethics & behaviour
• Personal/ social behaviour
• Values & attitudes
• Human rights
• Controversies
• Questions
• Concerns
• Global issues

Open-ended

People, places & practices
(How do people practise what they believe?)
• Leaders
• Festivals
• Special times
• Home life
• Places of worship
• Ordinary people
• Artefacts
• Rituals
• Customs

Key principles
• Education *not* instruction
• Inclusive *not* exclusive
• Open *not* closed
• Moving from the known to the unknown
• Diversity awareness – within as well as between religions
• More than just knowing facts
• Encouraging critical thinking

• Opportunities to reflect – personal learning and emotional development
• A balance between thematic and systematic teaching/learning
• Respect for the integrity of:
  – the children
  – the teacher
  – the religion/belief

What about confessional/faith teaching?
• should only be by consent
• must be explained to others
• must never be secret or mysterious
• is best at home and in the community.

awareness of religion as a local and global reality. It raises three
key questions:

- What do people believe?
- How do people practise what they believe?
- How do beliefs affect daily life and behaviour?

These questions should be explored in an inclusive manner in order
to develop understanding, sensitivity and critical openness, with
an appropriate balance between systematic teaching and thematic
approaches. The different strands should not just be about content
or 'knowing facts', but should also provide a basis for reflection and
emotional development while remaining open-ended and inclusive.
This has often been expressed in terms of the balance between
'learning *about* religion' and 'learning *from* religion' (see Grimmitt
2000), and such a model has been influential in other parts of the UK
and Europe.

This is not intended as a prescriptive model or as the only possible
alternative to the current structure. Perhaps its greatest value is that
it is a template which could be adapted and developed according to
identified needs in a particular school or group of schools. It proposes
a soundly educational alternative to the confessional and often
confused approach evident in the Core Syllabus. It offers a basis for
enabling shared schools (or schools that wish to extend their capacity
as shared spaces) to explore religious issues openly and fairly while
encouraging mutual respect. Additionally the set of guidelines in
Appendix 1 offers some key principles on which such an approach to
teaching RE might be based.

5 Uncomfortable issues

Any proposals for the broadening out of Religious Education are likely to raise issues and concerns in relation to the traditional expectations about RE in Northern Ireland. These relate especially to the place of confessional teaching in schools and the legal provision for withdrawal from RE classes.

Confessional teaching

The traditional assumption that publicly funded schools should provide religious teaching in the form of faith formation for children from a specific religious community seems to many people increasingly hard to sustain in the context of a plural global society. Such an approach fails to prepare children for the realities of life together in a very diverse but shared world, and at its worst it leads to the rigid separation of children into different confessional camps during a very formative period in their lives. One would like to think that those schools in Northern Ireland that are committed to a 'faith formation' approach – Catholic maintained schools and a small number of independent Protestant schools – would be making a special effort to ensure that separate religious teaching is offset by the inclusion of a broadly based religious curriculum and opportunities for significant inter-school cross-community encounter, but with a few exceptions this appears to be wishful thinking. It would also be a great shame if these expectations about 'faith-based' RE were to inhibit schools taking part in collaborative programmes from including RE in their plans.

In the view of the present writer, confessional teaching is a role for the Churches or other faith communities, not for the publicly funded school. In the UK and Ireland many Christian denominations and local parishes or congregations have done a relatively poor job in their church-based Christian Education programmes, whether for children or adults, because it has been assumed that this is taking place in schools. It is surely time for the various Churches to get their act together for this task *within* their own communities – and, better still, even in co-operation with each other – rather than to continue to place unrealistic expectations on the state-funded schools. This would release RE in schools from these inappropriate confessional pressures and free them up to develop a truly educational approach to teaching religion; it might also be a very healthy development for the Church communities themselves.

Nevertheless, this is not a position which can be reached quickly and thus for the present even those schools that are seeking to provide for children from a diversity of faith backgrounds will probably have to make some provision for an element of confessional teaching. In Northern Ireland the most obvious expression of this is in relation to the expectation that primary schools will prepare Catholic children for the sacraments of Reconciliation, First Communion and Confirmation.

Integrated schools have put considerable energy into reassuring Catholic parents that they can do this just as well as the Catholic schools, which is understandable. The situation does, however, raise issues about how to ensure that RE as a whole remains as inclusive as possible. The 'necessity' of dividing classes in order to provide confessional teaching about the sacraments, or of separating mixed classes *only* for RE, could be seen to undermine the very central principle of shared education. There is also the very practical issue of what to do for the other children while the Catholics are thus engaged. Attempts to provide parallel programmes for 'non-Catholic' children (as for instance in NICIE's *Delving Deeper* programme for Protestant children, referred to above) have proved difficult and elusive, and it is surely unwise to imply that the only alternative to a specifically Catholic form of RE is one that is specifically Protestant.

Under these circumstances it will be most important to ensure that all children do as much as possible of their RE *together* and that the content of RE is not assumed to begin and end with that which is denominationally specific to Catholic and Protestant forms of Christianity. Under no circumstances should the catechetical teaching appear secretive or mysterious to the other children, and every effort should be made to explain to those not personally involved what is being done. Those integrated schools that make the First Communion or Confirmation a shared celebration for all pupils, of all faiths and none, have spoken warmly of the value of such sharing.

This fundamental point is very clearly expressed in the Statement of Principles of the Northern Ireland Council for Integrated Education. It states that an integrated school: 'aspires to create an environment where those of all faiths and none are respected, acknowledged and accepted as valued members of the school community' (NICIE 2009). Elsewhere NICIE has proposed that:

> *In a school which is committed to making specific faith provision for its pupils, events and activities should, as much as possible, be inclusive rather than exclusive. In relation to the RE curriculum, children should only learn apart that which it would be unreasonable to ask them to learn together* **(NICIE 2008: 22).**

Withdrawing children from RE

A further contentious issue relates to the legal right of withdrawal from RE – a concession which goes back well over a century but which is not available in relation to any other subject.

In Northern Ireland, as in some other countries, parents have a legal right to request the withdrawal of their children from RE classes, and schools have an obligation to provide appropriate alternative work. Similarly, teachers may also request not to teach Religious Education on grounds of conscience. Research with parents from minority faith communities (Richardson 2003b) indicated that some families from such groups, but by no means all, do make a request for withdrawal. In that study and in a more recent study of attitudes and practice in relation to 'opting out' of RE (Mawhinney et al 2010), some families reported that schools did not tell them about their rights in this regard and some indicated that the process of exercising this right had proved extremely difficult. In practice in Northern Ireland relatively few parents (and even fewer teachers) avail of this possibility, but if it is requested all schools must respect the request and are legally obliged to facilitate it.

Difficulties in providing practical, properly supervised alternative arrangements have often made nonsense of the right of withdrawal.

There are many accounts of children sitting at the back of a class 'reading a book' but obviously listening to what is going on and often wanting to take part. In other schools the option of 'sitting outside the principal's office' provides an uncomfortable ambiguity about a child's absence from class. Some children undoubtedly feel very unhappy about being singled out in this way, especially if teachers are less than sensitive to the needs and feelings of children who withdraw from RE.

The greatest difficulty, however, is an ethical one. The right to withdraw strongly implies that in RE a particular religious position is being promoted, and this makes it much harder to persuade parents from a diversity of backgrounds that RE should be open, inclusive and genuinely educational.

Schools wishing to be as inclusive as possible in their RE teaching need to build the trust of parents, especially those from minority faith communities or non-religious backgrounds. Parents *can* be encouraged to participate and not to withdraw, but this will require careful explanation, patience, individual negotiation and – perhaps most of all – sensitive but clear leadership. Schools wishing to teach RE in an educational and inclusive manner will surely wish to pursue such an approach, while yet respecting the wishes of parents who may still remain unsure or in need of greater confidence.

Prayer in the classroom

Leaving aside the issue of school assembly for worship (the provision of which, like RE, is a legal requirement placed on schools),[10] prayer in primary classrooms (during RE lessons or saying grace before break or lunch) often takes place in a range of school types in Northern Ireland. This is particularly common in Catholic schools where it is probably expected by parents to be a key element of a school's RE programme, but in other kinds of schools it raises questions and uncertainties. Should children who are not from a Christian or other religious background be asked to take part in a religious practice, however simple and brief? Should parents have the right to ask for their children to be withdrawn from such situations? Or are those

10   This is too big a topic for discussion here, though many of the principles outlined in this document may well also apply to that issue.

who complain just a small, awkward minority who fail to recognise the strong Christian character that is still a characteristic of Northern Ireland? Much of this discussion relates closely to the other 'uncomfortable issues' outlined above.

Schools should discuss these issues and not leave them to chance or individual preference on the part of particular class teachers and a shared staff policy is highly desirable. It seems only fair that parents should be informed if such practices are to be permitted and they (and even the children) should be allowed to decide if they wish to take part.

Closely related to this is the practice by some teachers of giving children a task as part of an RE lesson to 'write a prayer' in response to a particular topic. When my student teachers ask if this is acceptable I always advise them that they should offer children an alternative – 'a prayer, or a poem, or a diary entry, or ...' – so that no one feels compelled to take part in an activity with which they would be uncomfortable. An alternative to this, perhaps with older pupils, would be to suggest: 'Write a prayer that a Christian [or whoever] might use about this issue'. In this way children may be able to appreciate the value of prayer to Christians, or other religious believers, without feeling that they have to conform, perhaps hypocritically, to practices that are not appropriate for them.

6 Concluding thoughts: the creative RE teacher

Religious Education has great potential as a vehicle for helping children and young people to develop awareness of and respect for religious diversity and to find creative and enriching ways of encounter with people who are from differing religious backgrounds. The role of the teacher is crucial in this process, and the teacher should be a model of such an approach. In their book *Religious Education in a Pluralist Society*, Hobson and Edwards raise this very question of the place of the teacher:

> *What are the desirable attitudes for a teacher of religious studies? ... Perhaps the most essential attitude would be one of openness to new perspectives and an ongoing interest in the search for truth (rather than a conviction that one already has all the answers). At the same time, a desire to assist others in the same search and to share one's doubts and questions would be highly desirable.*
> **(Hobson and Edwards 1999: 170-1)**

The creative teacher of RE, with children of whatever age group and from whatever background, will be an encourager of pupil enquiry, of curiosity and exploration. In such a teacher's classes, pupils will be motivated to articulate ideas and feelings and be able to reflect on their own and others' experiences. Classroom dialogue and exchange will be valued highly and adequate time will be made for interactive activities and discussion, based on critical thinking and an expanding knowledge and understanding. First-hand experience will be emphasised through the provision of opportunities to visit a range of relevant faith places and to receive visitors or engage in various kinds of encounters with people from different religious and cultural communities. Local and global perspectives on religion and other life stances will be developed, with an awareness of both similarities and differences. Within such an ethos some aspects of religion will be explored in a broadly thematic manner, especially with younger children, while other aspects will be explored more systematically, especially with older pupils.

This approach to RE already exists in some schools, though in too many others it is stultified because of the constraints, anxieties or hesitations indicated in the first part of this paper. Those who are convinced of the value of the open and genuinely educational study of religion in schools have the task of persuading their colleagues to shed the negative perceptions and engage with an altogether different way of doing RE. Schools venturing into collaborative relationships with partner schools from a different cultural and religious background, far from avoiding the perceived discomforts of shared RE, would surely find such an approach enlightening and enriching.

It may be that those schools that have already made a commitment to shared education, along with integrated schools, will wish to develop a syllabus for RE which reflects this approach, supported by appropriate training structures. Such a syllabus may yet become a model for other schools which are looking for broader alternatives to the Church-dominated programme as represented by the current Northern Ireland Core Syllabus. Whether a new kind of syllabus eventually emerges from the formal integrated sector or from elsewhere, the modelling of such an approach will surely do a great service to RE in all kinds of schools and will be of particular benefit in situations where children from different backgrounds are being taught together. The challenge will be to show that such an approach can be effectively implemented and that it can enrich our understanding, educationally, culturally and within and between our divided and diverse communities.

Appendix 1
Teaching RE inclusively: suggestions and guidelines for teachers

The premise of these guidelines is that it is possible for teachers of all religious backgrounds and of none, specialists and non-specialists, to teach RE with a clear conscience, both personally and professionally, and to offer some suggestions that may help. **The basic principle is to find an approach which respects the background of the pupil, the integrity of the teacher and the nature of the subject matter** (i.e. the religion or religions being studied). Most of these principles can apply in situations where the teacher is teaching pupils who all come from the same religious-cultural-ethnic background as well as situations where there are pupils from a range of backgrounds together in the same classroom.

- Be true to your own beliefs and insights. Like any other subject, RE fundamentally requires you to be first and foremost a good, professional teacher. It should not require you to sacrifice any personal beliefs or principles or to attempt to pretend that you are something that you are not.
- If you are not personally religious, don't be tempted to leave the teaching of RE to those with strong religious views. An *educational* approach to RE requires that children experience a breadth of views and approaches. No one has a monopoly of religious understanding.
- Where possible RE should include material on the religion which is most familiar to the children being taught and also on other, less familiar beliefs and practices. The expansion of pupils' horizons is very important, especially where there has been religious division and conflict. Rather than only reinforcing already held beliefs, good RE should surely be challenging children and young people to think.

- RE requires an approach which is sensitive to the various religious (or non-religious) viewpoints that may be represented by the pupils, their parents and the school community in general, but don't be over-cautious to the extent of failing to be adventurous. Keep parents well informed and even involve them if possible.
- Use inclusive language which emphasises your professional educational approach. For example, rather than phrases that imply that there is only one way of 'correct' belief, use expressions such as:
    - 'Some people think that ... while others think ...'
    - or 'Christians/Jews/Muslims, etc. believe ...'
    - or even (occasionally) 'I believe ... but others ...'.
- RE can be an ideal opportunity for encouraging the development of respect for differences and for building mutual understanding, especially in a society with a history of religious division. Don't just leave this to chance!
- RE is about helping pupils to explore their feelings and to develop personal attitudes and values. This requires a spirit of openness to their own ideas and goes beyond just giving them facts and information.
- RE involves knowledge and understanding, but it also relates to the human quest for meaning in life. Teachers can also enter into that quest and explore it with the pupils, whose insights can often be enlightening! (Children and young people need to know that adults are still learning, thinking, growing, exploring ... !)
- Make full use of the range of religious (or religious-related) festivals and special times which punctuate the year. They provide lots of material for a broadly based, multidisciplinary and intercultural approach to RE and provide a natural starting point for the exploration of religious practices, beliefs and issues.
- Confidence-building classroom strategies, such as Circle Time, which is based around emotional development, promoting trust and respect and the sharing of ideas in an open and democratic manner, can be an excellent way of dealing with the feelings, values and morality aspects of RE for all age groups.

- Agree principles and ground rules for discussion, especially for topics and issues that may involve sensitivities and deeply held beliefs. (See Figure 3 below.)
- RE can be taught in a broadly cross-curricular way, using approaches relating to a wide range of other skills and subjects - story (reading and writing); discussion; listening skills; drama; art; music; geography; history; science ..... and much else. Make the most of your own skills and interests in the way you develop topics and themes.

Figure 3: Ground rules for religious discussion

BE OPEN
Share your ideas and express your feelings.

BE HONEST
Say what you mean and mean what you say.

LISTEN!
... at least as much as you talk.

BE FAIR
Speak only for yourself and respect the right of others to think differently.

Appendix 2
Initiating a staff development process for the renewal of RE

Schools wishing to develop their Religious Education along the lines suggested here will need to engage all staff in discussion and consideration of an appropriate curriculum and practical arrangements. For such an approach to work it will require professional ownership by teachers and a supportive ethos of respect for diversity. Time for staff development is therefore crucial, and where schools are involved in shared education projects this should surely be done together with the whole staff (primary) or departmentally (post-primary) from all partnering schools.

A staff development day (or half-day) on this theme might have the following structure:

- in advance – an opportunity to read this document or a similar statement about sharing and diversity in Religious Education
- guided reflection and discussion on personal professional experiences of RE (see suggested reflection points below, under Discussion 1)
- feedback
- input, drawing on curriculum audits, inspection reports or other experiences (possibly involving a guest speaker)
- discussion towards proposing aims and ways of implementing a more inclusive approach to RE (see suggested discussion questions below – Discussion 2)
- feedback and agreement on practical steps that could be taken over the next months and into the next academic year.

Discussion 1: Guided reflection on experiences of teaching RE

If the situation is purely one of personal study, then the reader may wish to take some moments to write down his or her own reflections on the following questions.

- Share one thing you have really enjoyed/appreciated about teaching RE and one thing which has frustrated or irritated you.
- Share any experiences of teaching or learning in relation to RE that has taken place in an integrated or otherwise shared setting.
- What benefits from RE would you expect or hope that children and young people would gain from learning together in a shared environment that they might not so easily gain from other kinds of schools/settings?
- How openly can you discuss religious diversity with:
  - your pupils?
  - your colleagues?

Discussion 2: Present practice and ways forward

Consider and evaluate how RE is developed and organised in the school at present (based on results of surveys, audits, inspection reports where available, personal experience, and so on). Share experiences and highlight good practice.

Questions for all schools:

- Who teaches RE? When is RE taught?
- What is working well? What is not working so well?
- What are our aims/purposes/intended outcomes in relation to RE?
- How strong is our personal and collective knowledge base about religious diversity, within Christianity and in relation to world faiths?
- How effectively do we respond to the sharper edges of religious diversity in schools, especially in relation to sectarianism and racism? Do our pupils have any opportunities for encounter and sharing with their peers from different religious or belief traditions?

- What do we need to do to improve practice – personally and as a staff or inter-staff team?

Questions specially for school collaborations or integrated schools:

- What should be the distinctive contributions of the shared/ integrated classroom to RE?
- If in an integrated primary school, when and how do children prepare for the sacraments? (What are other children doing during this time?)
- Should there be a specific RE syllabus devised for integrated schools or shared school settings? What should it include?
- What opportunities are there – or should there be – for staff training and development to meet the needs of these situations?

Appendix 3
Education and religion: perspectives from human rights

Human rights instruments are widely regarded as internationally accepted standards by people of many different beliefs and backgrounds. Some of the key human rights statements on the relationship between religion and education are noted below.

According to Article 18 of the *Universal Declaration of Human Rights* (United Nations 1948), everyone has the right to freedom of thought, conscience and religion, including the right to change his/her religion or belief and to manifest that religion in teaching, practice, worship and observance. The universal right to education is affirmed by Article 26, which states:

> *Education shall be directed to the full development of the human personality and to the strengthening of respect for human rights and fundamental freedoms. It shall promote understanding, tolerance and friendship among all nations, racial or religious groups, and shall further the activities of the United Nations for the maintenance of peace.*

The right to freedom of thought, conscience and religion, and to freedom of expression, are also stated in the *European Convention on Human Rights and Fundamental Freedoms* (CoE 1950) which, in Article 9, also affirms the right of people to change and to manifest their religion (so long as the rights and freedoms of others are protected).

Clarifications of these rights have been delivered through the issuing of 'Protocols' at various stages since the original document was published. Article 2 of *Protocol No. 1* (1952) of the European Convention is often cited in relation to the responsibility of states for educational provision, and indicates that 'the State shall respect the right of parents to ensure such education and teaching in conformity with their own religions and philosophical convictions'. This has been interpreted by some as support for the teaching of religion only according to the parents' confessional convictions; others have understood it to mean that states cannot force children to receive teaching that is, for example, antagonistic to a particular faith or anti-religious (as, for example, in a totalitarian state). This is a matter that continues to require much greater clarification, though there are some suggestions of this in later statements, as indicated below.

In the *Declaration on the Elimination of All Forms of Intolerance and Discrimination based on Religion and Belief* (United Nations 1981), Article 5 states that:

> *every child shall enjoy the right to have access to education in the matter of religion or belief in accordance with the wishes of his parents ... and shall not be compelled to receive teaching on religion or belief against the wishes of his parents ... the best interests of the child being the guiding principle.*

In the same Article, however, a more inclusive tone is set by the statement that children 'shall be brought up in a spirit of understanding, tolerance, friendship among peoples, peace and universal brotherhood, respect for freedom of religion or belief of others'.

Many of these same principles were further upheld in the *Convention on the Rights of the Child* (United Nations 1989). Article 28 emphasised the importance of equal opportunity in education and stressed the need for international co-operation in education towards the elimination of ignorance. For educators the most significant statements are found in Article 29, which indicates that the purpose of education is to develop 'the child's personality, talents and mental and physical abilities to fullest potential'. It is also proposed that education should teach children to respect their parents, their own and others' cultures and should prepare them to live responsibly and peacefully in a free society, 'in the spirit of understanding, peace, tolerance, equality of sexes, and friendship among all peoples, ethnic, national and religious groups and persons of indigenous origin'.

Two very relevant statements to this discussion were issued in 2001 by means of United Nations consultative conferences. A 'Programme of Action' was set out at the *World Conference Against Racism, Racial Discrimination, Xenophobia and Related Intolerance* (United Nations 2001a) in which states were urged to adopt and implement

> *effective measures and policies ... which encourage all*
> *citizens and institutions to take a stand against racism,*
> *racial discrimination, xenophobia and related intolerance ...*
> *maximize the benefits of diversity within and among all nations*
> *... through public information and education programmes*
> *to raise awareness and understanding of the benefits of*
> *cultural diversity.*
> (Paragraph 59)

The second of these emerged from the Final Document of the *International Consultative Conference on School Education in Religion with Freedom of Religion and Belief* (United Nations 2001b). This important statement notes that 'tolerance involves the acceptance of diversity and respect for the right to be different, and that education, in particular at school, should contribute in a meaningful way to promote tolerance and respect for the freedom of religion and belief' and makes several pertinent recommendations:

- the need to 'promote through education the protection and respect for freedom of religion and belief in order to strengthen peace, understanding and tolerance, with a view to developing respect for pluralism' (Paragraph 1)
- that each state should 'promote and respect educational policies aimed at strengthening the promotion of human rights , eradicating prejudices ... and ensuring respect for and acceptance of pluralism and diversity in the field of religion or belief' (Paragraph 4)
- that each state should also promote and respect 'the right not to receive religious *instruction* inconsistent with his or her conviction' (Paragraph 4 – author's emphasis) [NB: the distinction that is

clearly made here by use of 'instruction' rather than 'education' is particularly significant in light of frequent public confusion between the two terms.]

- that those engaged in teaching should be encouraged to 'cultivate respect for religions or beliefs, thereby promoting mutual understanding and tolerance' (Paragraph 7b)
- that teachers and students should be provided with 'voluntary opportunities for meetings and exchanges with their counterparts of different religions or beliefs' (Paragraph 10d)
- that states and concerned institutions should consider 'studying, taking advantage of and disseminating best practices on education in relation to freedom of religion or belief, which attach particular importance to tolerance and non-discrimination' (Paragraph 12).

In 2007 the Office for Democratic Institutions and Human Rights (ODIHR) of the Organisation for Security and Co-operation in Europe (OSCE) established an Advisory Council of Experts on Freedom of Religion or Belief. This international group of lawyers, educationists and human rights experts produced the *Toledo Guiding Principles on Teaching About Religions and Beliefs in Public Schools* (OSCE/ODIHR 2007), which summarised its work in ten Key Guiding Principles, including the following paragraphs:

P.1   Teaching about religions and beliefs must be provided in ways that are fair, accurate and based on sound scholarship. Students should learn about religions and beliefs in an environment respectful of human rights, fundamental freedoms and civic values.

P.4   Efforts should be made to establish advisory bodies at different levels that take an inclusive approach to involving different stakeholders in the preparation and implementation of curricula and in the training of teachers.

P.6   Those who teach about religions and beliefs ... need to have the knowledge, attitude and skills to teach about religions and beliefs in a fair and balanced way. Teachers need not only subject-matter competence but pedagogical skills so that they can interact with students and help students interact with each other in sensitive and respectful ways.

P.7 Preparation of curricula, textbooks and educational materials for teaching about religions and beliefs should take into account religious and non-religious views in a way that is inclusive, fair, and respectful. Care should be taken to avoid inaccurate or prejudicial material, particularly when this reinforces negative stereotypes.

Over a number of years the Council of Europe, which represents 47 European states, has engaged in consultations in relation to ways of teaching about religion interculturally and with due regard for the protection of human rights. In 2008 the Committee of Ministers adopted a recommendation entitled *Dimensions of Religions and Non-Religious Convictions Within Intercultural Education: Recommendation CM/Rec(2008)12* (CoE 2008b). It advocated intercultural dialogue as 'an essential precondition for the development of tolerance and a culture of "living together"' and proposed that education should develop 'intercultural competences' through various means, including:

- providing opportunities to create spaces for intercultural dialogue in order to prevent religious or cultural divides
- promoting knowledge of different aspects (symbols, practices, etc.) of religious diversity
- combatting prejudice and stereotypes based on difference, which are barriers to intercultural dialogue, and teaching respect for equal dignity of all individuals.

Taken together, these ideals, principles and proposals can support educators in the development of a clear rationale and a practical strategy towards an inclusive and shared approach to the teaching of Religious Education.

Appendix 4
A glossary of key terms in RE

Catechesis

Christian teaching designed to instruct believers (especially young or new believers) in Christian faith and doctrine. The term originally referred to oral teaching but is now used more generally. It is related to the word 'catechism' – statements of Christian doctrine designed to be learned (by heart) – a term which is familiar in Catholic and some Protestant traditions, but in Ireland 'catechesis' is most often associated with Catholic practice.

Confessional RE

The teaching of religion in a way that is intended to promote a particular faith position or to nurture learners (who may be presumed to be believers) in that faith. It may also be understood simply as the teaching of religion from within a faith position. The term is sometimes used of a particular denominational approach (e.g. Catholic confessional teaching) and sometimes of more generic approaches (e.g. Christian confessional RE – or Muslim, Jewish, etc.)

Core syllabus

The Northern Ireland Core Syllabus is intended to be at the heart of RE but does not preclude the teaching of other material. The term was devised mainly in order to encourage Catholic and Protestant denominations to work together on a syllabus for RE while allowing Catholic

schools to teach additional denominational
material, as is their custom. (From time
to time the Department of Education has
encouraged schools to teach topics 'beyond
the core', particularly to extend the coverage
of world religions.)

Denominational RE   The teaching of RE according to the beliefs
and doctrines of a particular Christian
denomination – e.g. Catholic, Presbyterian,
etc. *Non-denominational* RE usually refers to
teaching that is generally Christian in nature
(and may therefore also be confessional) but
not specific to any single denomination or
tradition. ('Non-denominational' has often
been used as a synonym for 'Protestant' RE.)

Faith formation   A term favoured in Catholic schools
to describe the faith-based process of
RE, whereby children are encouraged
and nurtured in the Catholic faith and
prepared for some of the engagements
and responsibilities of its practice –
e.g. preparation for the sacraments of
Reconciliation, First Communion and
Confirmation (as in Catholic primary schools
in Northern Ireland).

Inclusive RE   In the context of this discussion 'inclusive
RE' refers to RE that is taught to all pupils,
of whatever belief background, together.
Inclusive RE is also about Catholics and
Protestants, and/or Christians and people
of other faiths and of no religion, learning
about and from each other in a spirit of
mutual respect.

Intercultural RE	RE that includes exploring and encountering diverse religions, beliefs and traditions; it implies not just 'knowing about' different beliefs but also using a range of interactive educational strategies to encourage understanding between them – discussion, meeting, visits, research, role-play, etc.
Non-denominational RE	*See entry on 'Denominational RE', above.*
Spiritual development	This is promoted in many educational systems, but it is often emphasised that it does not necessarily refer to religion. One of the most helpful definitions in the context of RE is that given by Mackley and Draycott (2004): 'Developing the qualities and dispositions which affect how we engage with life; how we relate to self, others, the world, and (for many) God, and an application of these in terms of values and beliefs'.

References and sources

Key books or articles on inclusive RE are in **bold.**

Chidester, D (2003) 'Religion Education in South Africa: teaching and learning about religion, religions and religious diversity', *British Journal of Religious Education,* 25 (4), Autumn 2003.

Churches' Working Party (2003) *Proposals for a Revised Core Syllabus in RE in Grant-Aided Schools in Northern Ireland,* Bangor, NI: Churches' Religious Education Core Syllabus Review Working Party.

CoE (Council of Europe) (1950) *European Convention on Human Rights and Fundamental Freedoms,* Strasbourg: Council of Europe Publishing. http://human-rights-convention.org/the-texts/the-convention-in-2010/

CoE (2008a) *White Paper on Intercultural Dialogue: Living Together as Equals in Dignity,* **Strasbourg: Council of Europe Publishing. http://www.coe.int/t/dg4/intercultural/source/white%20paper_ final_revised_en.pdf**

(CoE 2008b) *Dimensions of Religions and Non-Religious Convictions Within Intercultural Education: Recommendation CM/Rec (2008)12.* Strasbourg: Council of Europe Publishing: https://wcd.coe.int/ViewDoc. jsp?id=1386911&Site=CM

Crozier, M (ed) (1989) *Cultural Traditions in Northern Ireland: Varieties of Irishness,* Belfast: Institute of Irish Studies, Queen's University.

Curriculum for Excellence Scotland (no date) *Curriculum for Excellence – Religious and Moral Education: Principles and Practice* www.curriculumforexcellencescotland.gov.uk (accessed 06.02.14).

Department of Education NI (2007) *Revised Core Syllabus for Religious Education*, Bangor, NI: Department of Education (available from http://www.deni.gov.uk/re_core_syllabus_pdf.pdf)

ETI (2000) *Evaluating Religious Education*, Bangor, NI: Education & Training Inspectorate, Department of Education: http://www.deni.gov.uk/inspection_services/inspection_related_publications/RE2000.pdf (accessed 06.02.14).

Greer, J and McElhinney, E (1985) *Irish Christianity: A Guide for Teachers*, Dublin: Gill & Macmillan.

Grimmitt, M (ed) (2000) *Pedagogies of Religious Education: Case Studies in the Research and Development of Good Pedagogic Practice in RE*, Great Wakering: McCrimmons.

Hay, D (1990) 'Widening Horizons: The Religious Education Teacher as Deindoctrinator', in J Hammond, D Hay et al, *New Methods in RE Teaching: An Experimental Approach*, Harlow: Oliver & Boyd.

Hobson, P R and Edwards, J S (1999) *Religious Education in a Pluralist Society: The Key Philosophical Issues*, London: Woburn.

Keast, J (ed.) (2007) *Religious Diversity and Intercultural Education: A Reference Book for Schools*, Strasbourg: Council of Europe.

Mackley, J and Draycott, P (2004) *A to Z: Practical Learning Strategies to Support Spiritual and Moral Development*, Birmingham: RE Today Services.

Mawhinney, A (2006) 'The opt-out clause: imperfect protection for the right to freedom of religion in schools', *Education Law Journal*, 7 (2), 102–15.

Mawhinney, A (2007) 'Freedom of religion in the Irish primary school system: a failure to protect human rights?' *Legal Studies*, 27 (3), September 2007, 379–403.

Mawhinney, A, Niens, U, Richardson, N and Chiba, Y (2010) *Opting Out of Religious Education: The Views of Young People from Minority Belief Backgrounds*, Belfast: Queen's University School of Law and School of Education.

Murray, A (2010) 'A whole school approach to diversity and mutual understanding: a primary school perspective,' in N Richardson and T Gallagher, *Education for Diversity and Mutual Understanding: the Experience of Northern Ireland*, Bern: Peter Lang AG.

NICIE (2002) 'Primary school questionnaire: a summary of findings', unpublished survey by the Religious Education Focus Group, Belfast: Northern Ireland Council for Integrated Education.

NICIE (2005) *Delving Deeper*, Belfast: Northern Ireland Council for Integrated Education.

NICIE (2008) *ABC: Promoting an Anti-Bias Approach to Education in Northern Ireland*, Belfast: Northern Ireland Council for Integrated Education.

NICIE (2009) *Statement of Principles*, Belfast: Northern Ireland Council for Integrated Education.

Norwegian Directorate for Education and Training (no date) *Curriculum for Religion, Philosophies of Life and Ethics*, Oslo: Ministry of Education and Research: http://www.udir.no/Stottemeny/English/ (accessed 06.02.14).

OFMDFM (2005) *A Shared Future: Policy and Strategic Framework for Good Relations in Northern Ireland*, Belfast: Office of the First Minister and Deputy First Minister.

OSCE/ODIHR (2007) *Toledo Guiding Principles on Teaching About Religions and Beliefs in Public Schools,* **Warsaw: Office for Democratic Institutions and Human Rights of the Organisation for Security and Co-operation in Europe.**

QCA (2004) *Non-Statutory National Framework for Religious Education,* London: Qualifications and Curriculum Authority and Department for Education and Skills.

REC (Religious Education Council) (2013) *A Review of Religious Education in England,* London: Religious Education Council for England and Wales.

Richardson, N (2003a) 'Religious diversity in Northern Ireland: questions and challenges for educators', paper given at the Educational Studies Association Ireland conference, St Mary's University College, Belfast, April 2003.

Richardson, N (2003b) 'Curricular, faith and pastoral issues for minority faith children in Northern Ireland schools: the views of their parents', paper given at the Northern Ireland Inter-Faith Forum Conference on Diversity, World Faiths and Education, November 2003.

Richardson, N (2006) 'Student teachers and Religious Education in Northern Ireland', research paper given at the 2006 conference of the Association of University Lecturers in Religion and Education, Stranmillis University College, Belfast, September 2006.

Richardson, N (2008) 'Student teachers' perceptions of primary Religious Education in Northern Ireland schools', research paper given at the 2008 conference of the Association of University Lecturers in Religion and Education, Homerton College, Cambridge, July 2008.

Richardson, N (2012) 'Religious Education in Primary Schools: Report on a Survey of Teachers in Northern Ireland', unpublished research report.

South African Department of Education (2003) *National Policy on Religion and Education*, Pretoria: Government Printers.

United Nations (1948) *Universal Declaration of Human Rights*, Herndon, USA: United Nations Publications. http://www.un.org/en/documents/udhr/)

United Nations (1981) *Declaration on the Elimination of All Forms of Intolerance and Discrimination based on Religion and Belief*, Herndon, USA: United Nations Publications. http://www.un.org/documents/ga/res/36/a36r055.htm

United Nations (1989) *UN Convention on the Rights of the Child*, Herndon, USA: United Nations Publications. http://www.unicef.org.uk/Documents/Publication-pdfs/UNCRC_PRESS200910web.pdf

United Nations (2001a) *World Conference Against Racism, Racial Discrimination, Xenophobia and Related Intolerance*, Herndon, USA: United Nations Publications. http://www.un.org/WCAR/

United Nations (2001b) *Consultative Conference on School Education in Relation with Freedom of Religion or Belief, Tolerance or Non-Discrimination: Final Report*. [The full document is printed as Appendix IV of the 'Toledo Guiding Principles' document (see OSCE/ODIHR, 2007, above) and also available at: http://www.hurights.or.jp/pub/hreas/5/18appendix2.pdf]

Other relevant books
Connolly, P, Smith, A and Kelly, B (2002) *Too Young to Notice? The Cultural and Political Awareness of 3–6 Year Olds in Northern Ireland*, Belfast: Community Relations Council.

Council of Europe (2006) *The Religious Dimension of Intercultural Education*, Strasbourg: Council of Europe.

Grimmitt, M (ed) (2010) *Religious Education and Social and Community Cohesion: Challenges and Opportunities*, Great Wakering: McCrimmons.

Jackson, R (2004) *Rethinking Religious Education and Plurality*, London: RoutledgeFalmer.

Jackson, R and McKenna, U (eds) (2005) *Intercultural Education and Religious Plurality*, Oslo: Oslo Coalition on Freedom of Religion and Belief.

Meijer, W, Miedema, S and Lanser-van dr Velde, A (eds) (2009) *Religious Education in a World of Religious Diversity*, Münster: Waxmann.

Richardson, N and Gallagher, T (eds) (2010) *Education for Diversity and Mutual Understanding: the Experience of Northern Ireland*, Bern: Peter Lang AG.

Rivett, R (ed) (2007) *A Teacher's Handbook of Religious Education*, 3rd edn, Birmingham: RE Today Services.

Websites and other useful sources of information and ideas:
BBC Schools Religion Website: http://www.bbc.co.uk/schools/religion/
Excellent resources for pupils and teachers.

European Forum for Teachers of Religious Education (EFTRE):
http://www.eftre.net/
Information on RE in a range of countries, plus information on conferences and other relevant events. Many resources for teachers and pupils, including downloadable materials, plus many relevant links.

National Association for Teachers of Religious Education (NATRE):
http://www.natre.org.uk/
A UK-wide professional body for RE teachers.

Oslo Coalition on Freedom of Religion or Belief: an international network of representatives from faith communities, non-governmental organisations, international organisations and academia, with the aim of promoting freedom of religion or belief and strengthening interfaith co-operation worldwide. Of particular relevance is its project on Teaching for Tolerance and Freedom of Religion or Belief. Many articles and links are available on the website: www.oslocoalition.org/html/project_school_education/

RE Northern Ireland: http://renorthernireland.blogspot.com
A regularly updated blog by James Nelson, providing news and information about RE-related events and publications relevant to RE teachers in Northern Ireland.

RE Online website: http://www.reonline.org.uk/
A very wide range of sources and resources for RE teachers in all kinds of schools and all age groups.

RE Today Services: A UK-based support organisation supporting RE in schools by providing ecumenical and interfaith resources and services to promote and enable inclusive and fully professional approaches to Religious Education in the UK. See the website and catalogue for full details: http://www.retoday.org.uk/